RELATION OF VIRGINIA

Relation of Virginia

A BOY'S MEMOIR OF LIFE
WITH THE POWHATANS
AND PATAWOMECKS

By

HENRY SPELMAN

Transcribed from the original manuscript,
edited, and with an introduction by

KAREN ORDAHL KUPPERMAN

NEW YORK UNIVERSITY PRESS

New York

NEW YORK UNIVERSITY PRESS
New York
www.nyupress.org

References to Internet websites (URLs) were accurate at the time of writing. Neither
the author nor New York University Press is responsible for URLs that may have
expired or changed since the manuscript was prepared.

Library of Congress Cataloging-in-Publication Data
Names: Spelman, Henry, 1595–1623, author. | Kupperman, Karen Ordahl, 1939–   editor.
Title: Relation of Virginia : an early American memoir / by Henry Spelman :
edited and with an introduction by Karen Ordahl Kupperman.
Description: New York : New York University Press, [2019] |
Includes bibliographical references and index.
Identifiers: LCCN 2018043710| ISBN 9781479835195 (hbk. : alk. paper) |
ISBN 9781479872213 (pbk. : alk. paper)
Subjects: LCSH: Virginia—History—Colonial period, ca. 1600–1775. |
Indians of North America—Virginia. | Spelman, Henry, 1595–1623. |
Powhatan Indians. | Potomac Indians.
Classification: LCC F229 .S77 2019 | DDC 975.5/01—dc23
LC record available at https://lccn.loc.gov/2018043710

New York University Press books are printed on acid-free paper, and their binding
materials are chosen for strength and durability. We strive to use environmentally
responsible suppliers and materials to the greatest extent possible in
publishing our books.

Manufactured in the United States of America

10 9 8 7 6 5 4 3 2 1

Also available as an ebook

CONTENTS

[v]

Beinge in displeasure of my frendes, and desirus
to see other cuntryes, After ~~sum weekes~~ three months
sayle, wch cam wth prosperus winds in sight
of Virginia, wher A storme sodenly arisinge
scaured our ~~ship~~ fleete, (wch was of 8
sayle,) eury shipp from other, putting
us all in great daunger for vij or viij
dayes togither. But ye storme then ceasing
our shipp called ye vnitye cam ye next morning
saffly to an anker at Cape Henry, ye dayes of
October 1609, Wher we found thre other
of our fleete, and about a senight after
thre more cam thather ~~also~~. The residue
~~All remayned~~
^Amongst wch was S^r thomas Gates and S^r
Gorge Summers Knights, ~~not~~ ^we wear ~~being~~ hard of
many monthes after our arivall.

ACKNOWLEDGMENTS

FIRST AND FOREMOST, I want to thank Sam Fore, Librarian of the Harlan Crow Library, who first approached me about doing an edition of Spelman's manuscript. My editor, Clara Platter, traveled to Dallas to make images of the manuscript pages, and this allowed me to transcribe it from the original. Mandy Izadi provided me with images of Henry's letter to his uncle, which is in the Bodleian Library.

I also thank the Hakluyt Society for permission to reproduce the portion of William Strachey's *Historie of Travell into Virginia Britania*, edited by Louis B. Wright and Virginia Freund, that contains Henry's conversation with Iopassus about the creation of the world in Genesis and the Patawomeck creation story.

After the mother is delivered of her child
& in sum feaw dayes after the kinsfolke
and neyburs beinge intreated ther unto, -
cums unto ye house: wher beinge assemblid
the father, takes the child in his armes.
and declares that his ~~name~~ shall be, as he
then calls him, wch dum ye rest of ye day
So highly mann is
is spent in feastinge, and dauncinge.,

Ther manner of ~~buriall~~ visitinge the sicke
wth ye fation of ther buriall if they dye;

When any be sicke among them ther
prestes ~~one~~ cums unto the partye whom he
layeth on the ground uppon a matt And
hauing a boule of water, sett betwene him
and the sicke partye; and a Rattle by it,
the priest knealinge by the sick mans side

INTRODUCTION

EUROPEANS WANTED TO KNOW as much as they could about America's Native people. It was not just idle curiosity; scholars believed they could gain understanding of the history of the world by looking at cultures they deemed primitive. And ordinary people wanted to understand how Americans' practices were similar to or different from what was considered normal in Europe. How were their societies organized? Did they have the rule of law? What was their religious worship? Were they nomadic, or did they live in towns? What did they eat, and how did they prepare their food?

Such knowledge was surprisingly hard to come by for English readers. Spanish venturers had stumbled on sophisticated and highly organized societies in Central

America a century before England's Jamestown colony was founded in 1607, and scholars had been sending back detailed descriptions of those cultures all that time. But knowledge about Algonquians along North America's East Coast was elusive.[1] Most reports were written after brief encounters, and could only describe the way Native leaders presented themselves. Some Natives had been brought to England and put on display, but onlookers knew only what they saw. What readers needed was an insider's account of Native life. Luckily, sixteen-year-old Henry Spelman was able to provide exactly that.

Henry was fourteen when he arrived in Virginia in 1609 and he, like other boys who came on the ships, was sent to live with the Powhatans, Pocahontas's people. Europeans involved in Atlantic enterprises intentionally deposited young boys with Native leaders. They were supposed to learn the language and culture of their host people so they could act as interpreters and go-betweens with an insider's knowledge of both sides. Often Native leaders gave young men in return, and their purpose

---

1 Algonquian refers to a related group of languages, like Romance languages in Europe, including Spanish, French, and Italian. The Natives all along the coast up to New England spoke languages of the Algonquian group. Other language groups to the north and west were Siouan and Iroquoian.

was the same: they wanted to know as much as possible about the newcomers.

Henry Spelman differed from the other boys in a way that is very important to us: he wrote about his experiences in Virginia, and his account gives us an unparalleled picture of Chesapeake Algonquian cultures. Other reports were written by adults, who saw these people as antagonists and possibly a very great threat to the English. Native leaders controlled what they saw and whom they met. Henry's position was totally different. He wrote from the viewpoint of a young adolescent who was treated as an adopted son by the leaders of the two groups he lived with: the Powhatans and the Patawomecks. He was able to write about daily life, relationships between genders and ages, and religion in a way no one else could.

Jamestown was on the southernmost of the rivers flowing into Chesapeake Bay. Most of the tribes in the region were clients of the paramount chief Wahunsenaca, whom the English called Powhatan or the Powhatan. His own people were the Pamunkeys, and the tribes within the paramount chiefdom were collectively referred to as the Powhatans. Powhatan sent his young daughter Pocahontas to accompany official embassies to Jamestown in the early years.

Henry lived in Powhatan's capital city with another English boy, Thomas Savage, for several months. But he was uncomfortable even though Henry said Powhatan was kind to him. Henry's memoir gives two different accounts of an episode where Powhatan sent him to Jamestown with a message suggesting he would provide food for the colonists if a party of English came to him. In fact, it was a setup and the party was attacked. Obviously Henry had a hard time writing about this, as is demonstrated by the two versions he wrote, and his position was increasingly uncomfortable.

A new window opened for Henry when the Patawomeck leader Iopassus visited Powhatan. Henry and Thomas and a German carpenter called Samuel decided to accept Iopassus's invitation and accompany him north to the Potomac, but Powhatan did not want them to leave him. Henry wrote that Thomas ran back and told Powhatan about their plans, even though he had originally seemed willing to go north. Samuel was killed by Powhatan's men who pursued the absconders and Thomas stayed with Powhatan, while Henry was able to make his way to the Potomac.

In his life with Iopassus Henry found the acceptance and affection that he had not found with the English or with Powhatan. He was clearly treated as a member of the chief's family and Iopassus spoke of his love for Henry. His account of life with the Patawomecks makes clear that Iopassus's wives were not happy about his station in their household, but Henry was content and he was able to observe the intimate details of life from birth to death and daily activities in between. He even learned their beliefs about the afterlife.

Despite his being a loved member of the chief's family, Henry was not a free agent. Just as Thomas had understood that he was required to return to Powhatan, Henry was not able to leave Iopassus until Capt. Samuel Argall found him on one of his frequent searches for food to keep Jamestown going and gave Iopassus copper in exchange for Henry's freedom.

Argall soon returned to London and Henry traveled with him, so he spent a year in England from July 1611 to July 1612. It was during this time that Henry wrote his *Relation*, and he probably did it at the direction of his uncle, Sir Henry Spelman. Sir Henry was a noted historian and public figure, and a founding member of the Society of Antiquaries, which is what historians were called in those days.

European intellectuals were keenly interested in knowing about the American Natives and their cultures, partly because these people, whose existence God had kept hidden from Europeans, might reveal much about the nature and trajectory of human life on earth and about God's intentions for humanity. Many believed that they might be descended from the Ten Lost Tribes of Israel. The knowledge that God had given Adam had been fragmented as peoples became dispersed over the earth. Now, with their ability to study the peoples, plants, and animals of the newly disclosed continents, intellectuals hoped that they might bring all that knowledge together again. Henry's memoir was broken up into categories that reflected these interests, and Sir Henry, looking over his shoulder as he wrote, probably suggested them. Only the final category, their pastimes, might have been Henry's own.

Scholars interviewed Henry while he was in England, and some of his knowledge was not in his *Relation*, but appeared in other places. William Strachey had arrived in Virginia in 1610. He returned to London in late 1611, so he and Henry were there at the same time. Strachey, who served as colony secretary, spent his time gathering information so that he could write about Virginia when he returned home. He interviewed Henry and recounted the story of Capt. Argall's visit and how, on Christmas Eve, Iopassus came on board Argall's ship. Iopassus saw a man reading a Bible and wanted to know about it. Argall had Henry explain the creation story as told in one of the book's illustrations, and then Henry translated as Iopassus described his own people's beliefs about the creation and the afterlife.

Samuel Purchas, a Church of England cleric who dedicated himself to collecting and publishing accounts of foreign travel, also interviewed Henry. He published an abbreviated version of the Patawomeck creation story, saying that he got it from "an English youth." A marginal note identifies the youth as Henry Spelman.

THE MANUSCRIPT

Henry Spelman's *Relation of Virginia* was first presented to the world in 1872, 260 years after he wrote it, and the print run comprised only fifty copies. It had turned up in the library of an English collector named Dawson Turner, and was sold at auction in 1859. James F. Hunnewell of Charlestown, Massachusetts, acquired it in 1871 through the efforts of Henry Stevens. As Hunnewell wrote, "Lest it sleep another sleep of ages," he "at once" made arrangements for its publication "under the care of his friend Mr. Stevens, with instructions to see it clothed in a garb befitting its birth and destination."[2]

Spelman's manuscript remained in the Hunnewell family until the beginning of the twenty-first century, when the New Haven bookseller William Reese tracked it down after a two-year search. And the Harlan Crow Library in Dallas acquired it from Reese in 2006. It includes many words or phrases that are crossed out, and others written above the line as insertions as well as marginal notes. The extensive editing makes Spelman's *Relation* look like a work in progress, which may help to account for its not being published at the time.

We have one other piece of writing from Henry Spelman, a letter he wrote from Virginia to his uncle appealing for aid in 1615. Comparison of the two manuscripts makes one thing quite clear: they are not in the same handwriting. If we assume that the letter was written by Henry, then the *Relation* manuscript, written in a much simpler hand closer to modern handwriting, must have been a copy made by a scribe or secretary in Sir Henry Spelman's employ.[3] The first page is numbered

---

2 *Relation of Virginia by Henry Spelman 1609* (London: Printed for Jas. F. Hunnewell at the Chiswick Press, 1872).

3 Henry's letter is written in Secretary Hand, a style of writing used by well-educated people. Jehan de Beau-Chesne published a manual with "Rules made by E. B. for children to write by" that showed the proper

220, so it may have been part of a notebook or common-place book. Contemporaries copied things they wanted to remember into their commonplace books.

The insertions and marginal notes are in the same hand as the main text. Perhaps Henry dictated his man-uscript to the scribe and then went over it and had him make corrections. The changes could only have been made by someone who had direct knowledge of the events, people, and places mentioned, so we can assume they represent Henry's experience.

This edition presents two versions of the *Relation*. The first, in modern spelling, omits the crossed-out ma-terial and puts the insertions into the text. Although the spelling is modernized, it preserves Henry's punctuation. The second offers the text as Henry wrote or dictated it with contemporary spelling and editing and shows all the cross-outs and insertions. Through it we can see him struggling to record accurately certain contentious episodes, such as conflict between Capt. John Smith and Capt. Francis West over a settlement at the falls of the James, 220v-221. Even more poignant is his rewriting of his own fatal involvement in the false invitation to the

way to hold a pen and all the different styles of handwriting. The first manual was published in 1571 and new and revised versions continued to appear through 1611.

Jamestown authorities to come and get corn that resulted in many English deaths, 221v-222, 238–238v.

The present edition also includes the interviews with Henry about the Patawomeck creation story that were published by Samuel Purchas in his *Purchas His Pilgrimage*, 2nd ed. (London, 1614) and appeared in William Strachey's *The Historie of Travell into Virginia Britania*, written in 1612, but not published until the nineteenth century.[4]

Although it was not in print, Strachey's account circulated in several manuscript copies at the time of its composition. Print publication was valued differently in the seventeenth century from the way we see it today. It was common for very important works to circulate among a chosen few in manuscript, and this "scribal publication" was seen as a higher form. Not only are Strachey's manuscripts carefully done, but they are accompanied by the engravings of Algonquian life made by the workshop of Theodor DeBry from the paintings done by John White, who had been in Roanoke; and the engravings are me-

---

4 William Strachey, *The Historie of Travaile into Virginia Britannia; expressing the cosmographie and comodities of the country, togither with the manners and customes of the people*, ed. R. H. Major (London: Hakluyt Society, 1849). The excerpt printed here is from William Strachey, *The Historie of Travell into Virginia Britania*, ed. Louis B. Wright and Virginia Freund (London: Hakluyt Society, 1953), 101–3.

ticulously hand-colored, a very expensive addition.[5] Important people associated with Sir Henry had access to Henry's memoir and to his interviews with Strachey and Purchas.[6] With this edition, modern readers have access to the memoir with all its deletions and insertions, and can imagine young Henry struggling to present his experiences and knowledge to his uncle's colleagues in a form they could understand and accept.

Karen Ordahl Kupperman

New York City

July 2018

5 David S. Lupher, personal communication.

6 Harold Love, *The Culture and Commerce of Texts: Scribal Publication in Seventeenth-Century England* (Amherst: University of Massachusetts Press, 1998). Three copies of Strachey's manuscript survive, and each is dedicated to a very important man: Henry Percy, Earl of Northumberland, now in the Princeton University Library; Sir Allen Apsley, Surveyor to the King's Navy, now in the Bodleian Library of Oxford University; and Sir Francis Bacon, now in the British Library.

Beinge in displeasuer of my frendes, and desiring
to see other cuntryes; After sum weekes three months,
sayle, we cam w prosperus winds in sight
of Virginia, whe A storme sodenly arisinge
scaured our ship fleete, (w was of xx
sayle) every shipp from other, putting
us all in great daunger for vij or viij
dayes togither. But y storme then ceasing
our shipp called y vnitye cam y next morning
saffly to an anker at cape Henry, y dayes of
October 1609, Wher we found thre other
of our fleete, and about a senight after
thre more cam theather also. The residue
Amongst w was S Thomas Gates and S
Gorge Summers Knights, the yeare not being hard of
many monthis after our ariuall.

Relation of Virginia

with Modernized Spelling

[220]⁷ Being in displeasure of my friends, and desiring to see other countries, After three months sail we came with prosperous winds in sight of Virginia where A storm suddenly arising severed our fleet, (which was of x sail) every ship from other, putting us all in great danger for vij or viij dayes together.⁸ But the storm then ceasing, our ship called the unity came the next morning safely to an anchor at Cape Henry the [blank] day of

---

7 Manuscripts often used folio numbers rather than page numbers. The right-hand side is recto, and the back is verso. The fact that 220 is the first number indicates that this was placed within a much larger book of manuscripts.

8 Arabic numerals, the number system we use today, were relatively new in England, and many people continued to use Roman numerals for most purposes. *x* is 10, *v* is 5, and *ı* or *j* is 1.

October 1609, Where we found three other of our fleet, and about a senight after three more came thither also.[9] The residue, Amongst which was Sir Thomas Gates and Sir George Summers Knights, were not heard of many months after our arrival.[10]

[220v] From Cape Henry we sailed up the River of Powhatan[11] & within 4 or 5 days arrived at Jamestown, where we were joyfully welcomed by our countrymen being at that time about 80 persons under the government of Capt Smith, The President.[12] Having here unloaded our goods and bestowed some senight or fortnight in viewing of the country, I was carried by Capt. Smith our President to the Falls, to the little Powhatan[13] where unknown to me he sold me to him for a town called

---

9 *Senight* is one week (seven nights). Cape Henry, named for the oldest son of the English king James I, is at the opening of Chesapeake Bay.

10 Residue here refers to the other, still lost, ships in the 1609 fleet. Sir Thomas Gates, a military veteran, was to be the new head of government in Jamestown; Sir George Somers, a large investor in the Virginia Company, was the fleet's admiral.

11 Although the English colonists originally called the river on which they landed the Powhatan River because almost all the tribes along the river were his clients, the newcomers soon renamed it the James in honor of the English king.

12 Captain John Smith was the president of the governing council, the equivalent of governor. A fortnight is two weeks.

13 The man Henry calls the little Powhatan was Parahunt, son of the Great Powhatan.

From Cape Henry we sayled up y Riuer of
Powahtan c:w in 4 or 5 dayes ariued
at James toune, wher we weare ioyfully
welcomed by our Cuntrymen being at
that time about 80 persons under the
gourment of Capt Smith, The Præsident
Haueinge heare unladed our goods & bestoued
sum senight of fortnight in vieing of the
cuntry. J was caried By Capt Smith
our Præsidant to y fales, to y litell Powha-tan
wher unknowne to me he sould me to
him for a toune cauled Powhatan and
                    him
leaueinge me w: y litte Powhatam, He
made knowne to Capt wesbe how he
had bought a toune for them to dwell
desireing that caplaine west would come & settle himself ther-
in whereuppon Capt weste goeinge w th
but caplaine Wyste haueing
Bycause he had bestowed cost to begine
(misliked it. and unkindnesse thereuppon ariseing betweene them)
a toune in another place J but Capt
                            replied
Smith at that time saying well (but
                                        yet

Powhatan[14] and leaving me with him the little Powhatan, He made known to Capt West how he had bought a town for them to dwell desiring that captain West would come & settle himself there in, but captain West having bestowed cost to begin a town in another place misliked it: and unkindness thereupon arising between them, Capt Smith at that time replying little but [221] afterward conspired with the Powhatan to kill Capt West, which Plot took but small effect, for in the meantime Capt Smith was Apprehended, and sent aboard for England.[15] Myself having been now about vij or viij dayes with the little Powhatan, who though he made very much of me giving me such things as he had to win me to live with him, Yet I desired to see our English and therefore made signs unto him to give me leave to go to our ship to fetch such things as I left behind me, which he agreed unto and setting himself down, he clapped his hand on the ground in token he would stay there till I returned. But I staying

---

14 The town of Powhatan was the birthplace of the paramount chief, the Powhatan.

15 Francis West was the brother of Thomas West, Lord de la Warr, who became governor in 1610. The colonists were convinced that gold and silver deposits existed beyond the falls of the James. At this point, they could not travel around the falls, but hoped that a town there would be the base for future attempts. The Arrohattocs, clients of Powhatan, did attack the settlement, but West survived. Before that attack, Smith's powder bag exploded, injuring him severely, on his trip back down the James, and he returned to England for treatment.

somewhat too long, at my coming back to the place where I left him I found him departed, whereupon I went back to our ship being still in the Falls and sailed with them to Jamestown, where [221v] not being long there, Before one Thomas Savage with 4 or 5 Indians came from the great Powhatan with venison to Capt. Percy, who now was president.[16] After the delivery thereof and [knowing] that he must return, he was loath to go without some of his countrymen went with him, whereupon I was appointed to go, which I the more willingly did, by Reason that vitals[17] were scarce with us, carrying with me some copper and a hatchet which I had gotten. Coming to the Great Powhatan I presented to him such things as I had which he took, using me very kindly.[18] And After I had been with him about 3 weeks he sent me back to our English bidding me tell them, that if they would bring their ship, and some copper, he would [222] freight her back with corn, which I having reported to our English and returning their answer to the King, He before their coming laid

16 George Percy was the brother of Henry Percy, the Earl of Northumberland. Many accounts mention that he was sickly, and he was not placed at the head of government until there was no one else of suitable rank available. This was the first meeting of Henry and Thomas.
17 Victuals, food.
18 Henry showed that he had already learned something about American diplomacy by choosing to take a hatchet and copper with him as gifts for the Powhatan.

plots to take them, which in some sort he effected, for xxvj [*above line:* or vij] they killed which came towards land in their longboat, and shot many arrows into the ship, which our men perceiving and fearing the worst, weighed anchor and returned. Now while this business was in action the Powhatan sends me and one Samuel a Dutchman To a town about xvj miles off, called Yawtanoone willing us there to stay for him.[19]

[238. *Henry's manuscript includes the following alternate account of the same events:*]

freight them back corn which I having reported to our English, and returning their answer to the Powhatan. Captain Ratcliffe came with a ship with xxiiij or xxv men to Orapax, and leaving his ship there came by barge with sixteen men to the Powhatan to Pamunkey[20] where he very courteously in show received them by sending them bread and venison in reward whereof Captain Ratcliffe sent him copper and beads

---

19 Several Germans came in the ship that carried Thomas in 1608. They were needed for their special skills and when Powhatan requested men to build him a European-style house, Capt. John Smith sent four of them to do the job. The colonists referred to them as Dutch, their attempt to render the word Deutsch.

20 The Pamunkey River was an offshoot of the York River to the north of the Chickahominy, Orapax's location.

and such like Then Powhatan appointed Capt. Ratcliffe a house for him and his men to lie in during the
time that they should traffic,[21] not far from his own
but above half a mile from their barge, and himself in
the evening coming to the house slenderly accompanied) welcomed him thither, And returned leaving the
dutch man, Savage, and my self behind him. The next
day the Powhatan with a company of Savages came to
Capt. Ratcliffe, and carried our English to their storehouse where their corn was to traffic with them, giving them pieces of copper and beads and other things.
[238v] According to the proportions of the baskets of
corn which they brought but the Indians dealing deceitfully by putting or bearing up the bottom of their
baskets with their hands so that the less corn might
fill them. The English men taking exceptions against
it and a discontentment rising upon it the king (departed taking me and the dutchman with him) conveyed himself and his wives hence, And presently a
great number Indians that lay lurking in the woods &
corn about began with an oulis and whoopubb[22] and
whilest our English men were in haste carrying their
corn to their ships the Indians that were hidden in

---

21 Traffic was a common word for trading.
22 Possibly howling and hubbub.

the corn shot the men as they passed by them and so killed them all saving one William Russell and one other who being acquainted with the country escaped to James town by land.[23]

[222, cont.] At his coming there we understood how all things had passed by Thomas Savage, as before is related, the King in show made still much of us yet his mind was much declined from us which made us [222v] fear the worst, and having now been with him about 14 or 15 weeks,[24] it happened that the King of Patawomeck came to visit the great Powhatan, where being a while with him, he showed such kindness to Savage, Samuel, and myself as we determined to go away with him. When the day of his departure was come, we did as we agreed and having gone a mile

23 John Ratcliffe's name was usually coupled with "alias Sicklemore," Sicklemore being his family's name. He had been in and out of the colony from the beginning and had been a troublesome member of the government. For an account of his death see George Percy, "A Trewe Relacyon of the procedeings and ocurrentes of momente which have hapned in Virginia, from the Tyme Sir Thomas Gates was Shippwrackte uppon the Bermudes Anno 1609 untill my departure owtt of the Cowntry which was in Anno Domini 1612," ed. Mark Nicholls, *Virginia Magazine of History and Biography* 113, no. 3 (2005): 247–48. William Russell, gent., arrived in 1608.

24 The 1872 transcription rendered this as "24 or 25 weeks," but comparison of the scribe's rendition of the numeral 1 in the date 1609 on the first page, and of the numeral 2 on 224v, makes clear that it should be read as 14 or 15.

or two on the way, Savage feigned some excuse of stay &
unknown to us went back to the Powhatan and acquainted
him with our departing with the Patawomeck. The Powhatan presently sends after us commanding our return:
which we refusing [not believing] went still on our way:
and those that were sent, went still on with us, till one of
them finding opportunity on a sudden struck Samuel with
an axe and killed him, which [223] I seeing ran away from
among the company, they after me, the King and his men
after them, who overtaking them held them, till I shifted
for myself and got to the Patawomecks' country.[25] With this
King Patawomeck I lived a year and more at a town of his
called Pasptanzie, until such time as a worthy gentleman
named Capt. Argall arrived at a town called Nacottawtanke,
but by our English called Camocacocke, where he understood that there was an English boy named Harry. He,
desiring to hear further of me, came up the river, which
the King of Patawomeck hearing, sent me to him and I
going back again brought the king to the ship, where Captain Argall gave the King copper for me, which he received.
Thus was I set at liberty and brought into England.[26]

---

25 Captain John Smith wrote that Pocahontas had intervened to save
Henry and help him get to the Potomac.
26 For a fuller description of this encounter see the excerpts from
William Strachey and Samuel Purchas.

[224] OF THEIR SERVICE TO THEIR GODS

To give some satisfaction to my friends and contentment unto others, which wish well to this voyage, and are desirous to hear the fashions of that country, I have set down as well as I can, what I observed in the time I was among them. And therefore first concerning their gods, you must understand that for the most part they worship the devil, which the conjurers who are their priests, can make appear unto them at their pleasure, yet nevertheless in every country they have a several Image whom they call their god.[27]

> *Margin: list of deities:* Caukewis
>
> Manato
>
> Taukinge souke
>
> Quia(c)quasack

As with the great Powhatan, he has an Image called Cakeus which most commonly stands at Yaughtaw-noone or at Orapax in a house for that purpose and with him are set all the Kings goods and presents that are sent him, as the Corn, and the beads are. But the Crown and

---

27 Europeans considered religious worship other than Christian to be devil worship.

To give sum satisffaction to my frends and content
ment unto others, wch with reed to this viage, and
are desirus to hear ye fashions of that cuntrye:
I have set doune as well as I can what I
observed in ye time I was amonge them, and
therfore first concerninge ther gods, yow must
understand that for ye most part thy worship
ye divell, wch ye couniurers who are ther
prests, can make apeer unto them at ther
pleasure, yet nevere ye less in every cuntry
they have a severall Image whom they call
ther god. As in the great Pawstan he hath
an Image called Cakeres wch standeth at
or at Oropikes in ye house for that purposse
Yetaromnana in one of ye Kinges houses and
wth him are sett all the Kings goods and
presents y^e are sent him as ye Coviine And y^e
Bedd wch ye Kinge of England Sent him, and
in theire houses are all ye Kinges ancessters Buried, In ye Patomecks cuntry they have an
other god whom they call Quioquascacke,
and unto this Images they offer Beades

and

Cautunni
Manato
Tackings sauks
Quioquascacke

Bed which the King of England sent him are in the gods house at Orapax, and in these houses are all the King ancestors and kindred commonly buried. In the Patawomecks' country they have an other god whom they call Quioquascacke, and unto their Images they offer Beads [224v] and Copper if at any time they want Rain or have too much, and though they observe no day to worship their god: but upon necessity, yet once in the year, their priests which are their conjurers with the men, woman, and children do go into the woods, where their priests make a great circle of fire in the which after many observances in their conjurations they make offer of 2 or 3 children to be given to their god if he will appear unto them and show his mind whom he desire. Upon which offering they hear a noise out of the Circle Nominating such as he will have, whom presently they take binding them hand and foot and cast them into the circle of the fire, for be it the King's son he must be given if once named by ther god, After the bodies which are offered are consumed in the fire and their ceremonies performed the men depart merrily, the women weeping.[28]

28 Other authors described a ceremony involving boys who were moving into adolescence that involved a long ordeal in the woods. Originally many thought some of the boys were sacrificed, but they later realized that this was a ritual marking the end of the boys' lives as children and the beginning of their new lives as adults. The women wept

[225] OF THE COUNTRY OF VIRGINIA

The country is full of wood in some parts, and water they have plentiful, they have marshy ground and small fields, for corn, and other grounds whereon their Deer, goats, and stags feed. There be in this country Lions, Bears, wolves, foxes, musk cats,[29] Hares. flying squirrels, called assapameek and other squirrels being all gray like coneys, great store of fowl, only Peacocks and common hens wanting; fish in abundance where on they live most part of the Summer time They have a kind of wheat called Locataunce[30] and Peas and Beans, Great store of walnuts growing in every place. They have no orchard fruits, only two kind of plums, the one a sweet and luscious plum long and thick in form and likeness of A Nut Palm, the other resembling a medlar But somewhat sweeter, yet not edible till they be rotten as ours are.

---

over the loss of their close relationship with their children. See Helen C. Rountree, *The Powhatan Indians of Virginia: Their Traditional Culture* (Norman: University of Oklahoma Press, 1989), 80–82.

29 Probably muskrats.

30 Probably maize, what Americans today call corn.

[225v] OF THEIR TOWNS & BUILDINGS

Places of Habitation they have but few for the greatest town have not above 20 or 30 houses in it. Their Buildings are made like an oven with a little hole to come in at, But more spacious within having a hole in the midst of the house for smoke to go out at. The King's houses are both broader and longer then the rest having many dark windings and turnings before any come where the King is. But in that time when they go a-Hunting, the women go to a place appointed before, to build houses for their husbands to lie in at night carrying mats with them to cover their houses with all, and as the men go further a-hunting the women follow to make houses, always carrying their mats with them. Their manner of their Hunting is this: they meet some 2 or 300 together and having their bows and arrows and every one with a fire stick in their hand they beset a great [226] thicket round about, which done, every one set fire on the rank grass, which the Deer seeing flees from the fire, and the men coming in by a little and little encloseth their game in a narrow room [space], so as with their Bows and arrows they kill them at their pleasure taking their skins which is the greatest thing they desire, and some flesh for their provision.

Places of Habitation they haue but feaw
for y greatest towne haue not aboue 20 or
30 houses in it, ther Buildinge are made
like an ouen to a litkll hole to cum in at
But more spatius to in haueinge a holi in
the midest of y house for smoke to goe out
at, The Kinges houses are both broader and
longer haueinge many darke windinges and
turninges before any cum wher the Kinges is, But
in that time when they goe a Huntinge y
weomen goes to a place apoynted before, to
biuld houses for ther husbands to lie in att
night carieinge matts to them to couer ther
houses to att, and as the men goes further
a huntinge the weomen follows to make
houses, alwayes carrieinge ther mattes to them
ther maner of ther Huntinge is thiss when
they mett sum 2 or 300 togither and
haueinge ther bowes and arrows, and euery one
with a fier stick in ther hand they besett a great

[226v] THEIR MANNER OF MARRYING

The custom of the country is to have many wives and to buy them, so that he which have most copper and Beads may have most wives, for if he takes liking of any woman he makes love to her,[31] and seeks to her father or kinsfolk to set what price he must pay for her, which being once agreed on, the kindred meet and make good cheer, and when the sum agreed on be paid she shall be delivered to him for his wife,[32] The ceremony is thus The parents bring their daughter between them—if her parents be dead then some of her kinsfolk, or whom it pleases the king to appoint (for the man goes not unto any place to be married, But the woman is brought to him where he dwells). At her coming to him, her father or chief friends joins the hands together and then the father or chief friend of the man Brings a long [227] string of Beads and measuring his arm's length thereof does break it over the hands of those that are to be married while their hands be joined together, and gives it unto the womans father or him that brings her, And so with much mirth and feasting they go together, When the King of the country

---

31 Woos her to gain her favor.

32 This is the reverse of the dowry system in Europe in which the bride's father endowed her with goods for her new husband.

The maner of maring

The custum of ye cuntry is to haue many wiues
and to bये them, so ye he wth haue most copper
and Beads may haue most wiues, for if he
taketh likinge of any woman he makes loue
to hir, and seeketh to hir father or kindsfolke
to sett what price he must paye for hir,
wch beinge once agreed on the Kindred meett
and make good cheere, and when ye sume
agreed on be payd she shall be deliuered
to him for his wife, The Cerimony is thus
The parents bringes their daughter betwene them
(if hir parents be deade then suche of hir
Kinsfolke, or whom it pleaseth ye King to
apoynt (for ye man goes not unto any
place to be maried But ye woman is brought
to him where he dwelleth) At hir cumminge
to him, hir father or cheefe frends joyns
the hands togither and then ye father or
cheef frend of ye man Bringeth a longe

string

will have any wives he acquaints his chief men with his purpose, who sends into all parts of the country for the fairest and comeliest maids out of which the King takes his choice giving their parents what he pleases. If any of the King's wives have once a child by him, he keeps her no longer but puts her from him giving her sufficient Copper and beads to maintain her and the child while it is young and then is taken from her and maintained by the King, it now being lawful for her being thus put away to marry with any other,[33] The King Powhatan, having many wives, when he goes a-Hunting or to visit another King under him (for he goes not out of his own country), [227v] He leaves them with two old men who have the charge on them till his return.

This Pasptanse was brother to Patawomeck.[34] It was my hap[35] to be left at one of the King Pasptanses Houses when he went to visit another King and two of his wives were there also. After the King's depar-

33 The Powhatans were matrilineal, which meant that Powhatan chose wives from the leading families of his client tribes. After she bore a child, the mother returned to her home and the child, once it was old enough to leave her, returned and grew up in the paramount chief's home. The expectation was that the child, once grown up, would rule the client tribe from which the mother came. Most chiefs were men, but women also sometimes ruled.

34 The Patawomeck was the principal chief of the Patawomecks. His brother Iopassus, with whom Henry lived, ruled the city of Pasptanzie.

35 Luck.

ture, one of them would go visit her father, her name
was Paupauwiske, and seeing me, willed me to go with
her and to take her child and carry him thither in my
arms, being a long journey from the place where we
dwelt, which I refusing she struck me 3 or 4 blows, but
I being loath to bear too much got to her and pulled her
down giving her some blows again which the other of
the Kings wives perceiving, they both fell on me beat-
ing me so as I thought they had lamed me, Afterward
when the King came home, in their presence I acquainted him how they had used me. The King without
further delay tooke up a couwascohocan, which is a kind
of paring Iron,[36] and struck at one of them [228] with
such violence, as he felled her to the ground in manner
dead. I, seeing that, fled to a Neighbor's house, for fear
of the Kings displeasure. But his wife coming again to
herself somewhat appeased his anger, so as understanding where I was by his brother, he sent me his young
child to still, for none could quiet him so well as myself,
and about midnight he sent for him again. The next day
morning the King was early up, and came to the house
where I was. Loath I was to see him, yet being come to
him, instead of his anger, I found him kind to me, asking

---

36 A paring iron was like a spade with a sharp edge.

me how I did, and whether I was afraid of him last night, because I ran away from him, and hid myself. I being by his speeches somewhat bolder, Asked him for his Queen. He answered all was well, and that I should go home with him, telling me he loved me, and none should hurt me. I, though loath, went with him, where at my coming the Queen looked but discontentedly on me. But hoping on the King's promise, I cared the less for others' frowns, knowing well that the King made the more of me in hope I should help him to some copper, if at any time our English came into those parts, which I often had promised him to do, and which was by Capt. Argall Bountifully performed.

[228v] HOW THEY NAME THEIR CHILDREN

After the mother is delivered of her child, within some few days after, the kinsfolk and neighbors being entreated thereunto, comes unto the house, where being assembled the father takes the child in his arms and declares that his name shall be, as he then calls him, so his name is, which done, the rest of the day is spent in feasting and dancing.

THEIR MANNER OF VISITING THE SICK
WITH THE FASHION OF THEIR
BURIAL IF THEY DIE

When any be sick among them, their priests comes unto the party whom he lays on the ground upon a mat. And having a bowl of water, set between him and the sick party; and a Rattle by it, The priest kneeling by the sick man's side [229] dips his hand into the bowl, which taking up full of water, he sups into his mouth, spouting it out again, upon his own arms, and breast, then takes he the Rattle, and with one hand shakes that, and with the other he beats his breast, making a great noise, which having done he easily Rises (as loath to wake the sick body, first with one leg, then with the other, And being now got up, he leisurely goes about the sick man shaking his Rattle very softly over all his body, and with his hand he strokes the grieved parts of the sick, then does he besprinkle him with water mumbling certain words over him, and so for that time leaves him, But if he be wounded, after these ceremonies done unto him, he with a little flint stone gashes the wound making it to run and bleed which he setting his mouth unto it sucks out, and then applies a certain root beaten to powder unto the Sore.

After the mother is deliuered of her Child
& in sum fewe dayes after the Kinsfolke
and naybors beinge intreated ther unto,
cums unto ye house: wher beinge assembled
the father, takes the Child in his armes.
and declares that his ~~name~~ shall be, as he
then calls him, w dum ye rest of ye day
is spent in feastinge, and dauncinge.,

So high ~~maner is~~

Ther maner of ~~Susciwitte~~ visitinge the sicke
~~in ye fation of ther buriall if they dye.,~~

When any be sicke among them ther
prestes ~~ion~~ cums unto the partye whom he
layeth on the ground uppon a matt And
hauing a boule of water, sett betwene him
and the sicke partye; and a Rattle by it,
The preast knelinge by the sicke mans side

[229v] If he dies his burial is thus: there is a scaffold built about 3 or 4 yards high from the ground and the dead body wrapped in a mat is brought to the place, where when he is laid thereon, the kinsfolk falls a-weeping and make great sorrow, and instead of a dole for him, (the poorer people being got together) some of his kinsfolk flings Beads among them, making them to scramble for them, so that many times divers [several] do break their arms and legs being pressed by the company. This finished, they go to the party's house where they have meat given them, which being eaten, all the rest of the day they spend in singing and dancing using then as much mirth as before sorrow.[37] Moreover, if any of the kindred's bodies which have been laid on the scaffold be so consumed as nothing is left but bones, they take those bones from the scaffold and putting them into a new mat, hang them in their houses, where they continue while [230] their house falls and then they are buried in the ruins of the house. What goods the party leaves is divided among his wives and children. But his house he gives to the wife he likes best for life; after her death, unto what child he most loves.

---

37 This dancing and mirth speeds the departed along to the land of joy Henry described in his interview with William Strachey.

[230v] THE JUSTICE AND GOVERNMENT

Concerning their laws my years and understanding, made me the less to look after because I thought that Infidels were lawless.[38] Yet when I saw some put to death I asked the cause of their offence, for in the time that I was with the Patawomeck I saw 5 executed—4 for murder of a child (id est) [that is] the mother, and two others that did the fact with her and a 4th for concealing it as he passed by, being bribed to hold his peace, and one for robbing a traveler of copper and beads, for to steal their neighbor's corn or copper is death, or to lie once with another's wife is death if he be taken in the manner.

THE MANNER OF EXECUTION

Those that be convicted of capital offences are brought into a plain place before the King's house where then he lay, which was at Pamunkey, the chiefest house he has [231] where one or two appointed by the King did bind them hand and foot, which being done, a great fire was

---

38 Henry is saying that his youth and lack of understanding had made him assume that American Natives had no laws.

Concerninge their lawes my years and understan
dinge, made mee the leffe to looke after
bycause y thought y Infidels wear lawles
yet when y saw sum put to death y asked
the caufe of their offences, for in the time
y was in y Labomecke y saw 5e executed
4 for murther of a childe did roft, y mother
and brother y did the fact to her and a
4 for concealing it as he paffed by, beinge
brided to hould his peafes and one for
robbinge a traveler of coper and beades
for to steale their nyburs corne or
copper is death, or to lye one to anothers
wife is death if he be taken in the
manner,

The manor of execution

Thos that be convicted of capitall offences
are brough into a playne place before y
Kinges house wher then he laye, wch was
at Comunkeys the chefest house he hath

made. Then came [23IV] the officer to those that should die, and with a shell cut off their long lock, which they wear on the left side of their head, and hangs that on a bow before the Kings house. Then those for murder were Beaten with staves till their bones were broken, and being alive were flung into the fire, the other for robbing was knocked on the head and being dead his body was burnt.

[23IV] THE MANNER OF SETTING THEIR CORN WITH THE GATHERING AND DRESSING

They make most commonly a place about their houses to set their corn, which if there be much wood, in that place they cut down the great trees some half a yard above the ground, and the smaller they burn at the root pulling a good part of bark from them to make them die, in this place they dig many holes which before the English brought them scavels and spades they used to make with a crooked piece of wood being scraped of both sides in fashion of a gardener's paring Iron.[39] They

---

39 Stripping the bark around trees kills them because it cuts off the flow of nutrients. A scavel was a small spade.

They make most commonly a place about their
howses to sett their corne, wch if ther be
much wood, in that place the cutt downe
the great trees sum half a yard aboue
the ground, and ye smaller they burne
att the roote pullinge a good part of bagh from
them to make them die, on this place
they digg many holes wth before the english
brought them sceneles and spades they
vsed to make it a crooked peece of woode
burne scraped of bothsides in fation of
a gardiners paring Iron. they put
in to thes holes ordinarily 4 or 5 cor
nels of their wheat and 2 beanes like
french beanes, wch when the wheat dos
growe vp hauinge a straw as bigg as
a came reede the beanes rime vp there
like our hopps on poles, the eare of y^e
wheat is of great bignes in lenght and

put in to these holes ordinarily 4 or 5 kernels of their wheat and 2 beans like french beans, which when the wheat do grow up having a straw as big as a cane reed the beans run up thereon like our hops on poles.[40] The ear of the wheat is of great bigness in length and [232] compass and yet, for all the greatness of it, every stalk has most commonly some four or five ears on it, Their corn is set and gathered about the time we use, but their manner of their gathering is as we do our apples—first in a hand baskets, emptying them as they are filled into other bigger baskets whereof some are made of the barks of trees, some of hemp which naturally grows there, and some of the straw whereon the wheat grows. Now after the gathering, they lay it upon mats a good thickness in the sun to dry & every night they make a great pile of it, covering it over with mats to defend it from the dew, and when it is sufficiently weathered they pile it up in their houses, daily as occasion serves wringing the ears in pieces between their hands, and so [232v] rubbing out their corn[41] do put it into a great Basket which takes up the best part of some of their houses, and all

40 Hops are vines whose flowers are used in making beer. What Henry calls "their wheat" is what modern Americans call corn.
41 Henry here describes the way women, by wringing and twisting the ears, caused the dried kernels to drop out.

this is chiefly the women's work for the men do only hunt to get skins in winter and do tew or dress them in summer.[42]

But though now out of order yet let me not altogether forget the setting of the King's corn, for which a day is appointed wherein great part of the country people meet who with such diligence work as for the most part all the King's corn is set [planted] on a day. After which setting the King takes the crown which the King of England sent him, being brought him by two men, and sets it on his head, which done the people go about the corn in manner backwards, for they going before, and the king following, their faces are always toward the King expecting when he should fling some beads among them which his custom is at that time to do making those which had wrought to scramble for them. But to [233] some he favors he bids those that carry his Beads to call such and such unto him unto whom he gives beads into their hand and this is the greatest courtesy he does his people. When his corn is ripe the country people come to him again and gathers, dries, and rubs out all his corn for him, which is laid in houses appointed for that purpose.

---

42 Tewing was preparing leather by scraping and anointing it.

THE SITTING AT MEAT

They set on mats round about the house, the men by themselves, and the women by their selves. The women bring to everyone a dish of meat, for the better sort never eats together in one dish. When he has eaten what he will, or that which was given him, for he looks for no second course, he sets down his dish by him and mumbles certain words to himself in manner of giving thanks. If any left, the women gather it up & either keep it till the next meal, or give it to the poorer sort, if any be there.

[234] THE DIFFERENCES AMONG THEM

The King is not known by any difference from other of the chief sort in the country, but only when he comes to any of their houses they present him with copper Beads or Victuals, and show much reverence to him

The priests are shaven on the right side of their head close to the skull, only a little lock left at the ear and some of these have beards. But the common people have no beards at all, for they pull away their hairs as fast as it grows. And they also cut the hairs on the right side of their head that it might not hinder them by flapping

The King is not Know by any differene from
other of ye sorte [~~other~~] sorb in ye cuntry but only
when he cums to any of their houses they
present him wth Coppex Beads or Vitall. and
shew much reuerence to him

The preest are shauen on ye right side of their
head close to the scull only a litle locke
leaft at ye eare and seem of their heair beards
But ye common proploe haue no beards at
all for they pull away their heirs as fast
as it growes And they also cutt ye heairs
on ye right side of ther heade that it
might not hinder them by flappinge
about their bow stringe, when they draw
it to shostt, But on ye other side they lett
it grow and haue a long locke hanginge
doune ther shoulder,

about their bow string, when they draw it to shoot, But on the other side they let it grow & have a long lock hanging down their shoulder.

[235] THE ARMOR AND WEAPON WITH DISCIPLINE IN WAR

As for Armor or discipline in war, they have not any. The weapons they use for offence are Bows and Arrows with a weapon like a hammer and their Tomahawks for defence which are shields made of the bark of a tree and hanged on their left shoulder to cover that side as they stand forth to shoot[43]

They never fight in open fields but always either among reed or behind trees, taking their opportunity to shoot at their enemies, and till they can nock another arrow they make the trees their defense

In the time that I was there I saw a Battle fought between the Patawomeck and the Massawomeck, their place where they fought was a marshy ground full of Reed.[44]

---

43 Henry may have misremembered when he said tomahawks were shields, because, as became apparent in later accounts, the word probably applied to the hammer-like weapon.

44 Massawomecks were an Iroquoian-speaking tribe living to the northwest of the Potomac, possibly in the Appalachian Mountains. They were much-feared raiders.

As for Armor or disipline in warr the haue
not any. The wepons they vse for offence
are Bowes and Arrowes, and their Tomahaucks
for defence wch are shilds made of the barke
of a tree and hanged on their left shoulder
to couer that side, as they stand forth
to shoote

They neuer fight in open fields but alwaye
ether amonge reede or behind trees takinge
their oportunitie to shoot at their enimies
and till they can nocke another arrow
they make the trees their defence

In ye time that I was there I sawe
a Battell fought betwene the Patomeck
and the Masomeck, their place where
they fought was a marish ground full
of Reede. Being in the cuntry of the
Patomecke the people of Masomeck
weare brought thither in Canoes w^{ch}

Being in the country of the Patawomeck, the people of Massawomeck were brought thether in Canoes, which [235v] is a kind of Boat they have made in the form of a Hog's trough, but somewhat more hollowed in, On Both sides they scatter themselves some little distance one from the other, then take they their bows and arrows and having made ready to shoot, they softly steal toward their enemies, Sometime squatting down and prying if they can spy any to shoot at, whom if at any time he so Hurts that he cannot flee, they make haste to him to knock him on the head. And they that kill most of their enemies are held the chiefest men among them. Drums and Trumpets they have none, but when they will gather themselves together they have a kind of Howling or Hubbub so [236] differing in sound one from the other as both parts may very easily be distinguished. There was no great slaughter of neither side, but the Massawomecks, having shot away most of their arrows and wanting Victuals, were glad to retire

[237] THE PASTIMES

When they meet at feasts or otherwise they use sports much like to ours here in England, as their dancing, which is like our darbysher Hornpipe. A man first and

When they meet at feasts or otherwise they
vse sproets much like to ours heare in
England as ther daunsinge, wᶜʰ is like
our darbysher Hornepipe a man and a
woman and so through them all, hang
all in a round, ther is one wᶜʰ stand in
the midest wᵗʰ a pipe and a rattell wᶜʰ
wᶜʰ when he beginns to make a noyes
al the rest geigells about wringe ther
neckes and stampinge on yᵉ ground

They vse beside football play, wᶜʰ women as
young boyes doe much play at. The men
neuer they make ther goales about
only they neuer fight nor pull one
another doune

The men play wᵗʰ a litel balls letinge
it fall out of that hand and striketh
wᵗʰ the tope of his foot, and he that ca
strike the ball furthest winns that they
play for.

then a woman, and so through them all, hanging all in a round, there is one which stand in the midst with a pipe and a rattle with which when he begins to make a noise all the rest Gigetts[45] about wringing their necks and stamping on the ground

They use beside football play, which women and young boys do much play at, The men never. They make their Goals as ours, only they never fight nor pull one another down.

The men play with a little ball, letting it fall out of their hand and strikes it with the top of his foot, and he that can strike the ball furthest wins that they play for.

---

45 In England, to jig it meant to dance in a jerky and lively way.

Relation of Virginia

with Original Spelling, Cross-Outs, and Insertions

Folio numbers and editorial insertions are in brackets.
Insertions above the line are in italics. Henry's own
parentheses, crossed out words, and underlinings are retained.

[220] Beinge in displeasure of my frendes, and desiring
to see other cuntryes, After ~~sum weekes~~, *three months*
sayle *we* cam with prosperus winds in sight of Virginia
wher A storme sodenly arisinge seavered our ship fleete,
(which was of x sayle) every shipp from other, puttinge
us all in great daunger for vij or viij dayes togither . But
the storme then ceasing our shipp called the unitye cam
the next morning saffly to an anker at Cape Henry the
[blank] daye of October 1609, Wher we found thre
other of our fleete, and about a senight after thre more
cam thether *also*. The residew ~~still remayned~~ Amongst
which was Sir Thomas Gates and Sir George Summers

Knights ~~who~~ *wear* not ~~beinge~~ hard of many monthes after our arrivall. /

[220v] From Cape Henry we sayled up the River of Powahtan & with in 4 or 5 days arived at James toune, wher we weare joyfully welcomed by our Cuntrymen be-inge at that time about 80 persons under the goverment of Capt Smith, The Presidant. Havinge heare unladed our goods and bestowed some senight ~~of~~ or fortnight in viewing *of* the cuntry, I was caried By Capt Smith our Presidant to the Fales, to the litell Powha*tan* where un-Knowne to me he sould me to him for a towne caled Powhatan and leavinge me with *him* the litle Powhatann, He made knowne to Capt weste how he had bought a towne for them to dwell *desireing that captaine West would come & settle himself there in*, ~~Whereuppon Capt. weste growing~~ grew ~~angrye~~ (*but captaine Weste having*) ~~Bycasue he had~~ bestowed cost to begine a town in an-other place (*misliked it: and unkindnesse betweene them thereuppon ariseing*) ~~But~~ Capt Smith at that time ~~saying~~ replieing littel ~~yet~~ (*but*) [221] afterward ~~wrought~~ *con-spired* with the Powhawtan to Kill Capt weste, which Plott tooke but smale effect, for in the ~~interim~~ *meane time* Capt Smith was Aprehended, and sent abord for England, myself haveinge binn *now* about vij or viij dayes with the litell Powhatan who *though he* made very

From Cape Henry we sayled vp y Riuer of
Powahtan & w in 4 or 5 dayes ariued
at James toune, wher we ware ioyfully
welcomed by our Cuntrymen beinge at
that time about 80 persons under the
gouerment of Capt Smith, The Prasident
Haueinge heare unladed our goods & bestowed
sum senight of fortnight in vizinge of the
cuntry. J was caried By Capt Smith
our Presidant to y Fales, to y litell Powhatan
wher vnknowne to me he sould me to
him for a towne culed Powhatan and
leauinge me w him y litle Powhatam, He
made knowne to Capt weste how he
had bought a toune for them to dwell
desireing that captaine weste would come & settle himself ther
in Whereupon Capt weste grewe angry
but captaine weste haueinge
Becauese he had bestowed cost to begine
(mislikzed it: and vnkindnesse thereupon ariseing betwene them)
a toune in another place) But Capt
Smith at that time replied farewell (but)
yet

much of me givinge me such thinges as he had to winn
me to live with him. ~~When~~ *Yet* I desired to see our english and therefore made ~~signes~~ *signes* unto him ~~to~~ to
give me leave to goe to our ship to feach such thinges
as I leafte behind me, which he agreed unto and settinge *himselfe* downe, he clapt his hand on the ground
in token he would stay *ther* till I returned. But I staying sumwhat to long, at my cumming (to the place wher
I leaft h[torn] ~~backe~~ I found him departed wheruppon
I went backe to our shipp beinge still in the Fales and
Sayled with them to James toune, wher [221v] not beinge long ther, Before one Thomas Savage with 4 or 5
Indians cam from the *great* Powhatan with venison to
Capt: Percye, who now was president. After the delivery
thereof and that he must returne he was loith to goe with
out sum of his cuntrymen went with him, wher uppon
I was apoynted to goe, which I the more willingly did,
by Reason that vitals were scarse with us, carriing with
me sum copper and a hatchet ~~with me~~ which I had gotten. ~~And~~ Cumminge to the Great Powetan I presented
to him such thinges as I had which he tooke, using me
very kindly, ~~setting this Savage and me at his own Table~~
~~messe~~. And After I had bin with him About 3 weekes
he sent me backe to our English bidding me tell them,
that if they would bring ther Ship, and sum copper, he

would [222] Fraught hir backe with corne, which I having reported to our English and returning ther answere
to the Kinge, He before their cumminge layd plotts to
take them, which in sum sort he effected, for xxvj *or vij*
they killed which cam towards Land in ther long boat,
and shot many arrows into the ship, which our men
perseyving and fearinge the worst, wayed anker and returned. Now whil this business was in ~~doinge~~ action the
Powhatan sends me and one Samwell a Duchman To a
towne about xvj miles of, caled Yawtanoone willinge us
ther to stay ~~till~~ *for him,*

[238. *Another version of these events is given in the last
pages of the manuscript:*]

[Top left margin:] M18 Lye together the Orop
　　fraught thim backe corn which I haveing reported to our English, and returneing their ans-
weare to the Powhatan. Captaine Ratcyliff came
with a shipp with xxiiij or xxv men *to* Orohpikes,
and leaving his shipp there came by barge with sixteen men to the Powhatan to Pawmunkey where
he very curtiously in shew received them by sending them bread and venison in reward whereof
Captaine Ratclyff sent him copper and beades and

such like Then Powhatan appointed Cap: Ratclyff
a house for him and his men to lye in during the
time that thei should ~~traff~~ traffique, not far from his
own *but above half a mile from ther barge* and himself in the evening comeing to the ~~???~~ *house slenderly*
accompanied) welcomed him thither, And *returned*
~~afterward Rat~~ leaving the dutch man, Savage, and
my self behinde him. The next day the Powhatan
with a company of Salvages *came* to Capt. Ratcliff,
and caried our English to their storehouse where
their corne was to traffique with them, gieveing them
peices of copper *and beads* and other things. [238v]
According to the proportions of the basketts of
corne which they brought but the Indians dealing
deceitfully by putting or beareing *upp* the bottom of
their baskets with their hands so that the lesse corne
might ~~serve to~~ fill them. The English men taking
exceptions against it and a discontentment riseing
uppon it the king conveyed himself and his wives
hence *departed taking me and the dutchman with*
him And *presently a great number Indians that lay*
lurking in the woods & corne about began ??? an ou-
lis and whoopubb whilest our English men were in
hast carieing their corne to their shipps the Indians that weare hidden in the corn shott the men as

they passed by them and soe killed them all saveing one William Russell and one other whoe being acquainted with the Cuntry escaped to James towne by land.

[222, cont.] *At* his coming there we understood how althinges had passed by Thomas Savage, as before is related, the Kinge in showe made still much of us yet his mind was much declined from us which made us [222v] feare the worst, and having *now* bin with him about 14 or 15 weeks, it happned that the Kinge *of Pasptan* of Patomeck cam to visitt the great Powetan, wher beinge a while with him, he shewed such kindnes to Savage Samuell and my selfe as we determined to goe away with him, when the daye of his departure was cum, we did as we agreed and havinge gone a mile or two on the way, Savage fayned sum exceuse of stay & un knowne to us went back to the Powetan and acquaynted him with our fleing *departing with the Patowomeck*. The Powetan presenly sends after us comandinge our returne: which we not believing *refusing* went still on our way: and thos that weare sent, went still on with us, till one of them finding oportunity on a sunden struck Samuell with an axe and killed him, which [223] I seing ran a way from a monge the cumpany, they after me, the Kinge and his

men after them, who overtake them heald them, till I
shifted for my self and gott to the Patomeckes cuntry,
with this Kinge Patomecke I lived a year and more *at a
town of his called Pasptanzie* until such time as an worthy gentilman named Capt: Argall arived at a towne cald
Nacottawtanke, {Margin: Natauahanc} but by our English called Camocacocke, wher he understood that ther
was an english boy named Harry, He desiringe to here
furthere of me cam up the river which the King *of Patomeck* hearinge sent me to him and I goinge back *agayn*
brought the kinge to ~~him~~ *the shipe*, wher capt: Argall
gave the Kinge ~~some~~ copper for me, ~~???~~ *which he receyved*
Thus was I sett ~~free~~ *at libertye* and brought into England.

[224] OF THEIR SERVIS TO THEIR GODS

To give sum satisfaction to my frends and contentment unto others, which wish well to this viage, and are
desirus to heare the fashions of that cuntrye: I have set
doune as well as I can, what I observed in the time I was
amonge them. And therfore first concerninge ther gods,
you must understand that for the most part they worship
the divell, which the couniurers who are ther preests, can
make apearr unto them at ther pleasure, yet never the

To giue sum satisfaction to my frends and content
ment vnto others, wch with well to this viage, and
are desirus to hear ye fashions of that cuntrye:
J haue set doune as well as J can what J
obserued in ye time J was amonge them, And
therfore first concerninge these gods, yow must
vnderstand that for ye most part thy worship
ye diuell, wch ye couniurers who are ther
priests, can make apeere vnto them at ther
pleasure, yet neuer ye less in euery cuntry
they haue a seuerall Jmage whom thy call
ther god, As in the great Lawstan he hath
an Jmage called Cakeres wch most comonly standeth at
or at Croykes in a house not that purpose
Yatarowmes in one of ye kinges heads and
to him are sett all the Kings goods and
presents y^t are sent him as ye Corne and
Beades wch ye Kinge of England sent home, and
in their houses are all ye Kinge ancesters Buried, Jn ye Patomecks cuntry thay haue an
other god whom they call Ausoquascacke,
and vnto their Jmages thay offer Beades
and

+ Cautanus
Manato
* Tauskanes scaks
Ausaquasacks

less in every cuntry they have a severall Image whom they call ther god. {*Marginal list of deities:* xCaukewis, Manato, xTaukinge souke, Quia(c)quasack.} As with the great Pawetan he hath an Image called Cakeus which *most comonly* stands at Yaughtawnoone *or at Oropikes in a house for that purpose* in one of the King's houses and with him are sett all the Kings goods and presents that are sent him, as the Corn and the *beades are.* And the *Crown &* Bedd which the Kinge of England sent him *are in the gods house at* into *oropikes*, and in theise houses are all the Kinge ancesters *and kindred commonly* commonly Buried, In the Patomecks cuntry they have an other god whom they call Quioquascacke, and unto ther Images they offer Beades [224v] and Copper if at any time they want Rayne or have to much, and though they observe no day to worshipe ther god: but upon necessitye, yet onc in the year, ther preests which are their coniurers with the people *men*, weomen, and children doe goe into the woods, wher ther preests makes a great cirkell of fier in the which after many observanses in ther= coniurations they make offer of 2 or 3=children to be given to ther god if he will apeare unto them and shew his mind whom he will have *desier.* uppon which offering they heare a voyse out of the Cirkell Nominatinge such as he will have, whome presently they take bindinge them hand and footte and cast them into *the circle of* the fier, for be it the Kinges sonne he must be given if onc named by ther god, After the bodies ~~which are offered~~ are consumed in the fier and their cerimonies performed the men depart merily, the weomen weeping,

[225] OF THE CUNTRY OF VIRGINIA

The cuntry is full of wood ~~and~~ *in* sum partes, and water they have plentifull, they have marish ground and *smale* fields, for corne, and other grounds wher on their Deare, goates, and stages feadeth, ther be in this cuntry Lions, Beares, wolves, foxes, musk catts, Hares, fliinge squirrels, {*Margin:* caled assapaneek} and other Squirels beinge all graye like conyes, great store of foule only Peacockes and common hens wanting fish in aboundance wher on they live most part of the Smmer time, They have a Kind of wheat caled Locataunce and Pease and Beanes, Great store of walnuts growing in every place. They have noe orchard fruites, only tow kind of plumbes the one a sweet and lussius plumbe long and thicke in forme *and liknes* of A Nutt Palme. the other resemblinge a medler But sumwhat sweeter yet not Etable til they be rotten as ours are. /

[225v] OF THEIR TOUNES & BIULDINGES

Places of Habitation they have but feaw for the greatest
toune have not above 20 or 30 houses in it, Their Biuld-
inge are made like an oven with a litell hole to cum in
at But more spatius with in havinge a hole in the midest
of the house for smoke to goe out at, The Kinges houses
are both broader and longer *then the rest* havinge many
darke windinges and *turnings* before any cum wher the
Kinge is, But in that time when they goe a Huntinge the
weomen goes to a place apoynted before, to biuld houses
for ther husbands to lie in att night cariinge matts with
them to cover ther houses with all, and as the men goes
further a huntinge the weomen ~~goes before~~ *followes* to
make houses, always cariinge their mattes with them ther
maner of ther Huntinge is thiss ~~when~~ they meett some 2
or 300 togither and havinge ther bowes and arrows *and*
every one with a fier ~~in~~ sticke in their hand they be sett
a great [226] thikett round about, which dunn every one
sett fire on the ranke grass ~~and~~ *which* the Deare Seinge
fleeth from the fier, and the menn cumminge in by a litell
and litle incloseth ther game in a narrow roome, so as
with ther Bowes and arrowes they kill them at their plea-
suer takinge their skinns which is the greatest thinge they
desier, and sume flesh for ther ~~Vitall Suppers~~ provision.

Places of Habitation they haue but feaw
for ye greatest towne haue not aboue 20 or
30 houses in it, ther Buildinge are made
like an ouen to a litill hole to cum in at
But more spathus to in haueinge a hole in
the midest of ye house for smoke to goe out
at, The Kinges houses are both broader and
longer, haueinge many darke windinges and
turninges before any cum wher the Kinge is, But
in that time when they goe a hunlinge ye
weomen goes to a place apoynted before, to
buld houses for ther husbands to lie in at
night cariinge matts to them to couer the
houses to all, and as the men goes further
a hunlinge the weomen follonge to make
houses, always carriinge ther matts to them
ther maner of ther Huntinge is thiss
they mett sum 2 or 300 togither and
haueinge ther bowes and arrows, and euyone
to a fier sticke in ther hand they bisett a great

[226v] THER MANER OF MARIING

The custum of the cuntry is to have many wives and *to* buye them, so that he which have most copper and Beads may have most wives, for if he taketh likinge of any woman he makes love to hir, and seeketh to hir father or Kindsfolk to sett what price he must paye for hir, which beinge onc agreed on the Kindred meett and make good cheere, and when the sume agreed on be payd she shall be delivered to him for his wife, The cerimony is thus The parents bringes ther daughter betwene them (if her parents be deade then sume of hir Kinsfolk, or whom it pleaseth the King to apoynt (for the man goes not unto any place to be maried But the woman is brought to him where he dwelleth). At hir cumming to him, her father or cheef frends joynes the hands together and then the father or cheefe frend of the man Bringeth a longe [227] stringe of Beades and measuringe his armes leangth therof doth breake it over the hands of thos that are to be married while ther handes be ioynned *together and* ~~he~~ gives it unto the woman father or him that brings hir, And so with much mirth and feastinge they go togither, When the Kinge of the cuntry will have any wives he acquaintes his cheef men with his purpose, who sends ~~for~~ into all partes of

The custum of y̆ cuntry is to haue many wiues
and to buye them, so y̆ he w̆ch haue most copper
and Beads may haue most wiues, for if he
tabeth likinge of any woman he makes loue
to hir, and seketh to hir father or kindsfolke
to sett what price he must paye for hir,
w̆ch beinge once agreed on the kindred meete
and make good cheere, and when y̆ sume
agreed on be payd she shall be deliuered
to him for his wife, The Cerimony is thus
The parents bringes thir daughter betwene them
(if hir parents be deade then sume of hir
Kinsfolke, or whom it pleaseth y̆ King to
apoynt (for y̆ man goes not unto any
place to be maried But y̆ woman is brought
to him where he dwelleth) At hir cumminge
to him, hir father or cheefe freends ioyns
the hands togither and then y̆ father or
cheef frend of y̆ man Bringeth a longe

string

the cuntry for the fayrest and cumliest mayds out of which the Kinge taketh his choyse given ther parents what he pleaseth. If any of the Kings wives have onc a child by him, he ~~never lieth with hir more~~ *keeps her no longer* but puts hir from him givinge her suffitient Copper and beads to mayntayn hir and the child *while it is younge and then* is taken from hir and mayntayned by the King~~s charge~~, it now beinge lawfull for her *being thus put away* to marry with any other, *Poetan* The Kinge *having many wives* when he goeth a Huntinge or to Visitt another Kinge under him (for he goeth not out of his own cuntry)

[227v] He leaveth them with tow ould men who have the charge on them till his returne. / It was my happ to be left at one of the Kings *Pasptanses* {*Margin:* This Pasptanse was brother to Patomek} Houses when he went to visett another Kinge and two of his wives wear ther also, after the Kings departure, one of them would goe visett her father, ~~whos~~ *hir* name was Paupauwiske, and seinge me, willed me to goe with her and to take hir child and carye him thether in ~~his~~ *my* armes, beinge a ~~long~~ days iouyrnye from the place wher we dwelt, ~~but~~ *which* I refusinge she strooke me 3 or 4 blows, but I beinge loith to beare to much gott to hir and puld hir doune giving hir sum blows agayne which the

other of the Kings wives perseyvinge, they both fell on me beatinge me so as I thought they had lamed me, Afterwarde when the King cam home in their presents I acquainted him how they had used me, The King with out furthur delay tooke up a couwascohocan, which is a kind of paringe Iron, and strooke at one of them [228] with such violenc as he feld hir to the ground in manor deade. I seinge that, fled to a Neyghburs house, for feare of the Kings displeasuer, But his wife cumming againe to hir self : sumwhat apeased his anger So as understanding wher I was by his brother, he sent me his younge child to still, for none could quiet him so well as my selfe, and about midnight he sent for him again, The next day morninge the King was erlye upp, and came to the house where I was: loith I was to see him, yet being cum to him instead of his anger, I found him Kind to me, asking me how I did, and whether I was affrayd of him last night, by cause I rann away from him, and hidd my selfe, I being by his speeches sumwhat boulder, Asked him for his Queene, He answered all was well, and that I should goe home with him tellinge me he loved me, and none ~~should~~ should hurt me. I though loith went with him, wher at my cumminge the Queene looked but discontentedly on me, But hoping on the Kinges promise, I cared *the* less for others frownes, knowing well that the

Kinge made the more of me in hope I should healpe him to sum copper, if at any time our english cam into those parts, which I often had promised him to doe, and *which* was by Capt: Argoll Bountifully performed.

[228v] HOW THE NAMES
THER CHILDREN

After the mother is delivered of hir child with in sum feaw dayes after the Kinsfolke and nayburs beinge intreated ther unto, cums unto the house: wher beinge assembled the father, takes the child in his armes, and declares that his name shall be, as he then calls him, *so his name is* which dunn the rest of the day is spent in feastinge and dauncinge. /

THEIR MANNER OF ~~BURIALL~~ *VISITINGE*
THE SICKE WITH THE FASHION OF
THER BURIALL IF THEY DYE,

When any be sicke among them, ther preestes ??? cums unto the partye whom he layeth on the ground uppon a matt And having a boule of water, sett betwene him and

After the mother is deluered of her child
& in sum few dayes after the kinsfolke
and neybors beinge intreated ther unto,
cums unto ye house: wher beinge assembled
the father, takes the child in his armes.
and declares that his name shall be, as he
then calls him, so high maun is w dum ye rest of ye day
is spent in feastinge, and dauncinge.

Ther manor of visitinge the sicke
n ye fation of ther buriall if they dye.

When any be sicke among them ther
prestes cums unto the partye whom he
layeth on the ground uppon a matt And
hauing a boule of water, sett betwene him
and the sicke partye; and a Rattle by it,
The prest kneelinge by the sick mans side

the sicke partye; and a Rattle by it, The preest kneelinge
by the sick mans side [229] dipps his hand into the boule,
which taking up full of watter, he supps into his mouth,
spoutinge it out againe, uppon his owne armes, and brest,
then takes he the Rattle, and with one hand shakes that,
and with the other he beates his brest, makinge a great
noyes, which havinge dunn he Easilye Riseth (as loith
to wake the sicke bodye, first with one legge, then with
the other, And beinge now gott up, he leaysurely goeth
about the sicke *man* shakinge his Rattle very ~~easily~~ *softly*
over all his bodye: and with his hand he stroketh the
grieved parts of the sicke, then doth he besprinkell him
with water mumblinge certayne words over him, and
so for that time leave him, But if he be wounded after
thes cerimonyes dunn unto him he with a litle flint stone
gasheth the wound makinge it to runn and bleede which
he settinge his mouth unto it suckes out, and then aplies
a certayn root *betten to powder* unto the Sore.

[229v] If he dies his buriall is thus ther is a scaffould biult about 3 or 4 yards hye from the ground and
the deade bodye wraped in a matt is *brought to the place,
where when he is* layd ther on, the Kinsfolke fales a weap-
inge and make great Sorrow, and instead of a dole for
him, (the porer people beinge gott togither) sum of his
Kinsfolke flinges Beades amonge them makinge them to

scramble for them, so that many times divers doe breake ther armes and legges beinge pressed by the cumpany, this finished they goe to the parties house wher they have meat given them which being AEten all the rest of the day they spend in singinge and dauncinge using *then* as much mirth as before sorrow more over if any of the Kindreds bodies which have bin layd on the scaffould be so consumed as nothing is leaft but bonns they take thos bonns from the scaffould and puttinge them into a new matt, hangs them in their houses, wher they continew whille [230] ther house falleth and then they are buried in the ruines of the house what goods the partye leaveth is devided amonge his wives and children. But his house he giveth to the wife he liketh best for life, after her death, unto what child he most loveth,

[230v] THE JUSTIS AND GOVERMENT

Concerninge ther lawes my years and understandinge, made me the lesse to looke after by cause I thought that infidels weare lawless yet when I saw sum put to death I asked the cause of ther offence, for in the time I was with the Patomecke I saw 5 executed 4 for murther of a child (id est) the mother, and tow other that did the fact with hir and a 4 for consealing it as he passed by, beinge bribed to hould his pease of and one for robbinge a traveler of coper and beades for to steale ther neybur's corne or copper is death, or to lye onc with anothers wife is death if he be taken in the manner. /

THE MANOR OF EXECUTION

Thos that be convicted of capitall offences are brough into a playne place before the Kinges house wher then he laye, which was at Pomunkeye the chefest house he hath [231] wher one *or two* apoynted by the Kinge did bind them hand and foote, which being dunn a great fier was made, Then cam the officer to thos that should dye, and with a shell cutt of ther long locke, which they weare on the leaft side of ther heade, and hangeth that on a bowe before the Kinge house Then thos for murther wear Beaten with staves ~~???~~ till ther bonns weare broken and beinge alive *weare* flounge into the fier, the other for robbinge was knocked on the heade and beinge deade *his* bodye was burnt.

[231v] THE MANOR OF SETTINGE THER CORNE WITH THE GATHERINGE & DRESSING.

They make most commonly a place about ther houses to sett their corne, which if ther be much wood, in that place the cutt doune the great trees sum half a yard above the ground, and the smaller they burne att the roote pullinge a good part *of bark* from them to make them die, in this place they digg many holes which before the English brought them scavels and spades they used to make with a crooked peece of woode beinge scrapsed of both sides in fation of a gardiners paring Iron. they put in to thes holes ordenarily 4 or 5 currnels of ther wheat and 2 beanes like french beanes, which when the wheat doe growe up havinge a straw as bigg as a canne reede the beanes runn up theron like our hopps on poles, The eare of the wheat is of great bignes in lenght and [232] cumpace and yet for all the greatnes of it every stalke hath most commonly sum fower or five eares on it, Ther corne is sett and gathered about the time we use, but ther maner of ther gatheringe is as we doe our ~~aplse~~ Appels first in a hand basketts ~~???~~ emtiing them as they are filled into *other* bigger basketts wherof sum are made of the barkes of trees, sume of heampe which naturally groweth ther, and some of the straw wheron the wheat groweth, Now after the gatheringe, they laye it uppon mats agood thicknes in the sonn to drye & every night they make a great pile of it, coveringe it over with matts to defend it from the dewe, ~~which~~ and when it is suffitienly weathered they pile it up in ther houses, dayly as occation serveth wringinge the eares in peices betwene ther hands, and so [232v] rubbinge out ther corne do put it in to a great Baskett which taketh upp the best parte of sum of their houses, and all this is cheefly the weomen's worke for the men doe only hunt to gett skinns in winter and doe tewe *or dress* them in summer.

But though now out of order yet let me not altogither forgett the settinge of the Kings corne for which a day is a poynted wherin great part of the cuntry people meete who with such diligence worketh as for the most part all the Kinges corne is sett on a daye After which setting the Kinge takes the croune which the Kinge of England sent him beinge brought him by tow men, and setts it on his heade which dunn the people goeth about the corne in maner backwardes for they going before, and the king followinge ther faces are always toward the Kinge expectinge when he should flinge sum beades amonge them which his custum is at that time to doe makeing

those which had wrought to scramble for them But to
[233] sume he favors he bids thos that carry his Beads
to call such and such unto him unto whome he giveth
beads into ther hande and this is the greatest curtesey he
doth his people, when his corn is ripe the cuntry *people*
cums to him *againe* and gathers drys and rubbes out all
his corne for him, which is layd in howses apoynted for
that purpose. /

THE SETTINGE AT MEAT

They set on matts round about the house the men by
them selves and the weomen by ther selves the weomen bringe to every one a dish of meat for the better
sort never eates togither in one dish, when he hath eaten
what he will, or that which was given him, *for* he looks
for no ~~next~~ second corse he setts doune his dish by him
and mumleth ceartayne words to him self in manor of
~~saying grace~~ givinge thankes, if any leaft the weomen
gather it up & ether keeps it till the next meall, or gives
it to the porer sort, if any be ther.

[234]⁴⁶ THE DIFFERENCES AMONG THEM

The King is not know by any differenc from other of the ~~better~~ *chefe* sort in the cuntry but only when he cums to any of ther howses they present him with Copper Beads or Vitall⁴⁷, and shew much reverence to him

The preest are shaven on the right side of ther head close to the scull only a litle locke leaft at the eare and sum of thes have beards But the common people have no beards at all for they pull away ther hares as fast as it growes And they also cutt the heares on the right side of their heade that it might not hinder them by flappinge about ther bow stringe, when they draw it to shoott, But on the other side they lett it grow and have a long locke hanginge doune ther shoulder. /

---

46 There is no folio 233v in the manuscript.

47 In the text, this appears to be written Vilatt, but it is clear from other instances on folio 226 and 236 that Vitall (victual) is intended. The scribe's letter *t* in the middle of a word is often not crossed, as in the word *litle* three lines down, and the scribe often makes a flourish through double *l*s that make them look like letter *t*s to modern eyes; see the last line on folio 220 and the words *all* and *Ratell* on folio 237.

The King is not Know by any differenc from
other of ye cheefe sort in ye cuntry but only
when he cums to any of ther houses they
present him wth Copper Beads or Vitall. and
shew much reuerences to him

The preest are shauen on ye right side of ther
head close to the scull only a litle locke
leaft at ye eare and sum of them haue beards
But ye common people haue no beards at
all for they pull away ther hares as fast
as it growes And they also cutt ye heares
on ye right side of ther heade that it
might not hinder them by flappinge
about ther bow stringe, when they draw
it to shott, But on ye other side they lett
it grow and haue a long locke hanginge
doune ther shoulder,

[235] THE ARMOR AND WEPON
WITH DISSIPLINE IN WAR

As for Armo*u*re or dissipline in ware the have not any.
The weopons they use for ~~offsene~~ *offence* are Bowes and
Arrowes *with a weapon like a hammer* and ther Tomahaucks for defence which are shilds made of the barke
of a tree and hanged on their leaft shoulder to cover that
side as they stand forth to shoote

They never fight in open fields but always ether
amonge reede or behind trees takinge ther oportunitie
to shoot at their enimies and till they can nocke another
arrow they make the trees ther defence

In the time that I was ther I sawe a Battell fought
betwene the Patomeck and the Masomeck, ther place
wher they fought was a marish ground full of Reede
Beinge in the cuntry of the Patomecke the peopel of
Masomeck weare brought thether in Canoes which
[235v] is a kind of Boate they have made in the forme
of an Hoggs trough But sumwhat more hollowed in,
On Both sids they scatter them selves sum litle distant
one from the other, then take they ther bows and arrows and havinge made ridie to shoot they softly steale
toward ther enimies, Sumtime squattinge downe and
priinge if they can spie any to shoot at whom if at any

the Armor and wepon
& the dissipline in war
235

As for Armoure or dissipline in war the have
not any. The weapons they vse for offence
are Bowes and Arrowes, and their Tomahauck's
for defence wch are shilds made of the barke
of a tree and hanged on ther laft shoulder
to coure that side, as they stand forth
to shoote

it is a wepon like a hammer

They neuer fight in open fields but alway
ether amonge reede or behind trees takinge
ther oportunitie to shoot at ther enimies
and till they can nocke another arrow
they make the trees ther defence
In yt time that I was ther I sawe
a Battell fought betwene the Patomeck
and the Masomeck, ther place where
they fought was a marish ground full
of Reede Being in the cuntry of the
Patomecke the propel of Masomeck
weare brought thither in Canoes wch

time he so Hurteth that he can not flee they make hast
to him to knock him on the heade, And they that Kill
most of ther enimies are heald the cheefest men amonge
them; Drums and Trumpetts they have none, but when
they will gather them selves togither they have a kind of
Howlinge or Howbabub so [236] differinge in sounde
one from the other as both part may very aesely be distinguished. Ther was no great slauwter of nether side
But the massomecks having shott a way most of ther arrows and - - - wantinge Vitall ~~was~~ *weare* glad to retier,

[237] THE PASTIMES

[Note: the extreme right side of this folio has been trimmed.]

When they meet at feasts or otherwise they use
sprorts much like to ours heare in England as their
daunsinge, which is like our darbysher Hornepipe a man
first and *then* a woman, and so through them all, hang
all in a round, ther is one which stand in the midest with
a pipe and a rattell with which when he beginns to make
a noyse al the rest Gigetts about wriinge ther neckes and
stampinge on the ground

They use beside football play, which wemen and
young boyes doe much play at. The men never They

when they meet at feasts or otherwise they
vse sproets much like to ours here in
England as ther daunsinge, wch is like
our darbyshire Hornepipe a man and a
woman and so through them all, hand in
all in a round, ther is one wch stand in
the midest wth a pipe and a rattell wth
wch when he begins to make a noyse,
all the rest gigetts about wringe ther
neckes and stampinge on y ground

They vse beside football play, wch women as
young boyes doe much play at. the men
neuer They make ther gooles about
only they neuer fight nor pull one
another downe

The men play wth a litel botle lettinge
it fall out of ther hand and striketh it
wth the tope of his foot, and he that can
strike the ball furthest winns that they
play for.

make ther Gooles as ours only they never fight nor pull one another doune

The men play with a litel balle lettinge it fall out of ther hand and striketh [*word trimmed*] with the tope of his foot, and he that can strike the ball furthest winns that they play for.

WILLIAM STRACHEY ON SPELMAN'S ACCOUNT OF THE PATAWOMECK CREATION STORY AND AFTERLIFE

I will conclude these points with opinion of the Indians of Patawomeck-river the last yeare 1610. about Christmas when Capt. Argoll was there trading with Iopassus the great kings brother, after many daies of acquaintance with him as the Pynnace road before the Towne *Mattchipongo,* Iopassus comming abourd and sitting (the weather being very Cold) by the fire upon a harth in the Hold with the Captayne, one of our men was reading of a Bible, to which the Indian gave a very attent eare and looked with a very wish't eye upon him as if he desired to understand what he read, whereupon the Captayne tooke the booke, and turned to the Picture

William Strachey, *The Historie of Travell into Virginia Britania* (1612), ed. Louis B. Wright and Virginia Freund (London: Hakluyt Society, 1953), 101–3.

of the Creation of the world, in the beginning of the book, and caused a Boy one Spilman, who had lived a whole yeare with this Indian-King, and spake his language, to shew it unto him, and to enterprett yt in his language, which the boy did, and which the king seemed to like well of: howbeit he bade the boy tell the Capt, yf he would heare, he would tell him the manner of their begynning, which was a pretty fabulous tale indeed: "We have (said he) 5. godes in all our chief god appeares often unto us in the likewise of a mightie great Hare, the other 4. have no visible shape, but are (indeed) the 4. wyndes, which keepe the 4. Corners of the earth (and then with his hand he seemed to quarter out the scytuation of the world) our god who takes upon this shape of a Hare conceaved with himself how to people this great world, and with what kynd of Creatures, and yt is true (said he) that at length he divised and made divers men and women and made provision for them to be kept up yet for a while in a great bag, now there were certayne spirritts, which he described to be like great Giants, which came to the Hares dwelling place (being towards the rising of the Sun and hadd perserveraunce of the men and women, which he had put into that great bag, and they would have had them to eate, but the godlike Hare reproved those Caniball Spirritts and drove them awaie. Nowe yf the boy had asked him of what he made those men and women and what those spirritts more particularly had bene and so had proceeded in some order, they should have made yt hang togither the better, but the boy was unwilling to question him so many things lest he should offend him, only the old man went on, and said, how that godlike hare made the water and the fish therein and the land and a greate deare, which should feed upon the land, at which assembled the other 4. gods envious hereat, from the east the west from the north and sowth and with hunting poles kild this deare drest him, and after they had feasted with him departed againe east west north and sowth, at which the other god in despight of this their mallice to him, tooke all the haires of the slayne deare and spredd them upon the earth with many powerfull wordes and charmes whereby every haire became a deare and then he opened the great bag, wherein the men and the women were, and placed them upon the earth, a man and a woman in one Country and a man and a woman in another country, and so the world tooke his first begynning of mankynd, the Captayne bade the boy aske him, what he thought became of them after their death, to which he answered somwhat like as is expressed before of the Inhabitants about us, howe that after they are dead here, they goe up to the toppe of a highe tree, and there they espie a faire plaine broad pathe waye, on both sydes whereof doth grow all manner of pleasant fruicts, as Mulberryes, Strawberryes, Plombes etc. In this pleasant path they run toward the rysing of the sun, where the godlike hares howse is, and in the midd waie they come to a howse, where a woman goddesse doth dwell, who hath alwaies her doores open for hospitality and hath at all tymes ready drest greene *Uskatahomen* and *Pokahichary* (which is greene Corne bruysed and boyld, and walnutts beatten smale, then washed from the Shells, with a quantety of water, which makes a kynd of Milke and which they esteeme an extraordinary dainty dish) togither with all manner of pleasant fruicts in a readines to entertayne all such as do travell to the great hares howse, and when they are well refreshed, they run in this pleasant path to the rysing of the Sun, where they fynd their forefathers living in great pleasure in a goodly feild, where they doe nothing but daunce and sing, and feed on delicious fruicts with that great Hare, who is their great god, and when they have lived there, untill they be starke old men, they saie they dye there likewise by turnes and come into the world againe.

SAMUEL PURCHAS ON HIS
INTERVIEW WITH SPELMAN

I may also here insert the ridiculous conceits which some Virginians hold, concerning their first originall, as I have heard from the relation of an English youth [margin: Capt Argoles boy his name was Henrie Spilman] which lived long amongst the Savages: that a Hare came into their Countrey and made the first men, and after preserved them from a great Serpent: and when two other Hares came thither, that Hare for their entertainment killed a Deere and that was then the only Deere that was, and strewing the haires of that Deere hide every haire proved a Deere. He said they worshipped towards a certaine Hoope or Sphere doubled a cross, which was set upon an heape of stones in their houses.

Samuel Purchas, *Purchas His Pilgrimage*, 2nd ed. (London, 1614), 767.